Welcome to Space Camp

by Mary Kate O'Day

PEARSON

Glenview, Illinois • Boston, Massachusetts • Chandler, Arizona
Upper Saddle River, New Jersey

Astronauts weigh less on the Moon.

In July 1969, two astronauts walked on the Moon. There, Neil Armstrong and Buzz Aldrin saw rocks everywhere. There was no air or wind. Neil and Buzz felt very light. They learned to walk on the Moon.

space shuttle

rockets

Rockets help spacecraft leave Earth's gravity.

To get to space, astronauts had to leave Earth's gravity.

Did You Know? **Gravity**

On Earth, gravity pulls things and people. It pulls them to the center of the Earth. This way, things and people do not float away. Spacecraft need rockets to get away from Earth's gravity. Rockets are strong machines. They push spacecraft into space.

At space camp, you can do what astronauts do.

Real astronauts get ready to go to space. They simulate the jobs they will do there. To simulate means to practice to do something.

At space camp, you can do simulation activities. These are like the activities done in space. You will feel what astronauts feel in space.

Did You Know? **Simulators**

Astronauts work in simulators on Earth. Simulators are machines. Astronauts use simulators to practice the things they will do in space.

The astronauts learn to stay alive in space. They learn how to move. They learn how to work. They learn how to eat and sleep.

There is very little gravity in space. Astronauts float in the air. They learn to work while floating in a simulator.

At space camp, campers use simulators.

Astronauts learn to eat in no gravity. Their food floats in the air. They need to catch it. Sometimes they squeeze food from a tube. It goes right into their mouths.

At space camp, you can do things in no gravity. You use a gravity chair. It makes you feel like you are on the Moon. In a simulator, you feel weightless. You float and walk like you are in space.

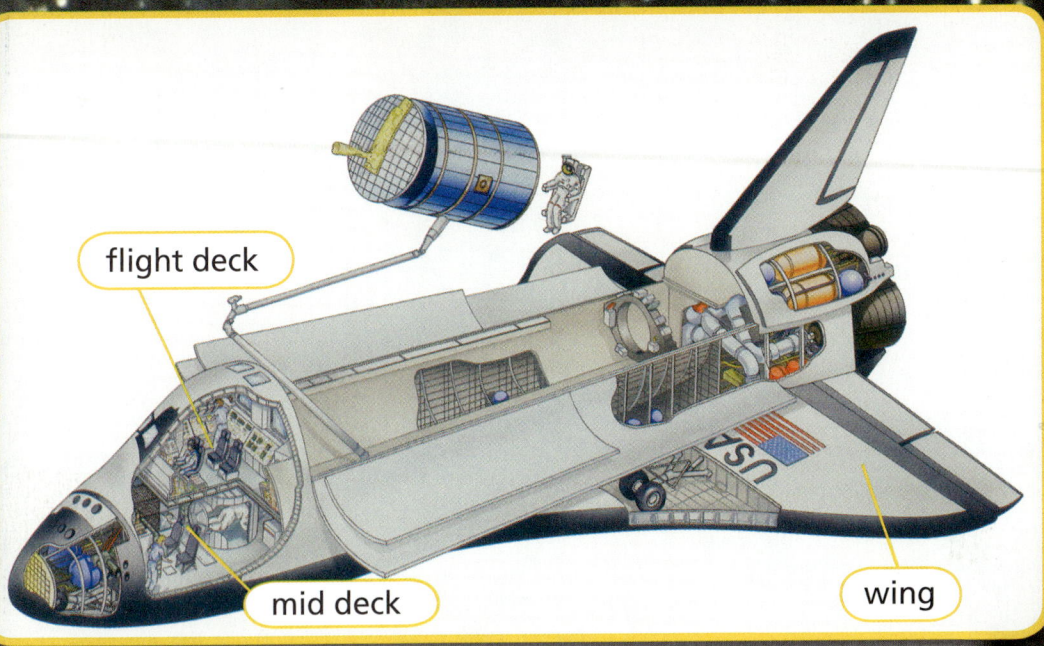

A space shuttle

Some space camps have a copy of a space shuttle. A space shuttle is a spacecraft with wings. You can go inside a copy at space camp.

Inside, you can see the flight deck. This is where astronauts control the spacecraft. You can see the mid deck. This is where a lot of work is done. You can learn about many jobs astronauts do.

Campers can also do a practice space mission. A mission is a trip where you do work. Campers work together on teams.

One team works in the control center. The control center is on Earth. Control center workers are important. They help the astronauts on the shuttle.

Another team works inside the shuttle. They work on machines. They make choices. They also do what they are told.

The teams at camp do work just like a real mission. The teams launch the spacecraft. They control it in space. They have many jobs to do. The teams do experiments to learn about space.

In the control center, the teams work together. They bring the shuttle back to Earth. This is why astronauts use simulators. Everything they learn, they do in space.

At some space camps, you can see real rockets. You can see real spacecraft. You learn about space history.

You may also learn about Galileo and Newton. These two men studied space long ago.

Shows like this help campers learn about space history.

Did You Know? Galileo and Newton

- Galileo was from Italy. He lived from 1564 to 1642. He improved telescopes. Telescopes let you see things that are far away. In 1610, Galileo found four moons near Jupiter.

- Sir Isaac Newton lived in England. He was born in 1642. He told people about gravity. He built a new telescope. He told people how the planets moved.

At space camp, you learn many things. You learn to eat and sleep in space.

You can also build small rockets. You learn to do experiments. You learn about being an astronaut.

Would you like to experience life in space? Space camp can help you do this. Maybe you will be an astronaut one day!